ENDOMOR PLAN

The Complete Guide to Loss that Excess Fat and Stay Healthy with Paleo Diet, Exercises, and Trainings Perfect for Your Body Type.
Includes Recipes and Meal Plan

Nancy Peterson
Copyright@2019

Table of Content

Introduction 3
Chapter 1 4
What is an Endomorph 4
Types of Bodies 5
Physical Characteristics of Endomorphs 6
Metabolic Characteristics 7
Chapter 2 8
How to Eat for an Endomorph Body Type 8
What should an Endomorph Eat? 9
Diet and Weight Loss 12
Best Choice for Breakfast 13
Chapter 3: Fitness Goals 15
Recommendations for Cardio Training for
Endomorphs 16
Explaining High-Intensity Interval Training (HIIT),
.... 16
Weight Training 21
Recommendations for Weight Training 22
Chapter 4 25
The Beginner's Guide to Paleo Diet 25
Setting Up A Paleo Diet Meal Plan 26
Foods to Avoid on the Paleo Diet 27

Foods to Eat on the Paleo Diet 28
A Paleo Menu Plan for One Week 32
Simple Paleo Snacks 35
Paleo Diet Shopping List 36
How to Make Restaurant Meals Paleo-Friendly .. 37
My Favorite Paleo Recipes 38
Chapter 4: Conclusion 118
Other Books by Nancy Peterson 119

Introduction

Can the Endomorph Diet Help with Weight Loss?

Are you trying to drop some excess pounds or just want to add some definition to your muscle? All you need to get results is to carry out regular exercises and sustain a healthy diet. However, having good success with diet and workout plans depends on your body type. While some diet and workout plan may work for you, some other diet plan may not work for you.

If the percentage of your body fat is high while your muscle definition is low, you may have what is called an endomorph body. Several people with endomorph bodies have had it tough with losing excess weight. The answer to this is simply understanding your body type and knowing what you should eat and what you shouldn't eat to fit your body type.

In this book, we will discuss how endomorphs can achieve their weight loss goals, with step by step instructions and directions.

Chapter 1

What is an Endomorph

In the 1940s, an American researcher and psychologist, William Sheldon, introduced the classification of the different body types. From his research, it was concluded that using our body composition and skeletal frame, every single individual has inherited different body types that determine if we are heavier, leaner, or somewhere in the middle of the two. Because we all have different body types, being able to achieve our weight loss and fitness goals will require a specialized plan that suits your body type.

Endomorph, according to William Sheldon, is a human body type that tends to be round. Endomorphs have less muscle mass and a higher percentage of body fat, making them rounder and heavier, but not necessarily obese.

In a normal situation, an endomorphic person has a lot of body fat, but should not be described as a fat person. Even if you do not eat as an endomorph, you may remain the same, just that you might be thinner. Because of the makeup of their body, individuals with endomorphic bodies are more concerned with their calorie intake than individuals with other body types. Endomorphs have to ensure that they do not eat more calories than they can burn.

Types of Bodies

We have three types of bodies, which are endomorphs, mesomorphs, and ectomorphs.

Endomorphs are to eat with caution so as not to consume more calories than their bodies can burn. Endomorphs have a larger frame and find it very difficult to shed weight, even when they decide to starve themselves.

These characteristics are what differentiates the endomorphs from the other two body types.

People with mesomorph somatotype are in between the ectomorph body and the endomorph body. They have a large skeletal frame, but they still have a lower percentage of fat in their body. They find it easy to gain muscle weight as much as they find it easy to shed weight.

People with ectomorph, on the other hand, have a higher metabolism, which means that no matter how much they eat, they gain only a little percent of weight. They also have a smaller body size, smaller joints, and a narrower frame.

Physical Characteristics of Endomorphs

Examples of popular female endomorphs are Jennifer Lopez, Marilyn Monroe, Beyoncé, and Sophia Vergara. You can describe them as having curves, a small waist, a full figure with a pear shape.

Endomorphs come with a smooth round body, have medium to large bone structure, short limbs, and small shoulders. Their weight usually rests on the lower abdomen, thighs, and hips rather than being distributed equally all over the body. Because of the way they are built, it makes it somehow too hard to shed weight, but when you use the right nutrition program and correct training, this will become possible.

Metabolic Characteristics

Looking at the endomorph body from a metabolic aspect, they are usually sensitive to insulin and carbohydrate. Foods with high carb count are easily converted to sugar in their bloodstream; this makes it possible for the body to store them as fat rather than being used to burn energy. Because of this, most endomorphic people tend to have a high body-fat percentage, which puts them at risk of developing infertility, diabetes, gallbladder conditions, some types of cancer, hypertension, heart diseases, and depression.

The good news is that these hormonal imbalances can be corrected or even prevented when you are on a nutrition and fitness program that would help reduce body fat.

Chapter 2

How to Eat for an Endomorph Body Type

When you take a look at people around you, you will notice that no two people have the same built. However, a closer look would show you some similarities in the shapes of their bodies. Like I stated earlier, most individuals fall under the three different body types: ectomorphs, mesomorphs, and endomorphs. Each of these body types has different diet plans and training methods to help individuals achieve their fitness, weight management, and overall health goals. Truly, most people may have a combination of two body types, but one of the body types always dominates the other.

Ectomorphs are lean and long and have a fast metabolism, which makes it hard for them to gain weight and develop muscles. Mesomorphs, on the other hand, are naturally muscular, and they find it easy to add or lose weight.

Our focus is on the endomorph who has a larger bone structure, finds it easy to store fat, and very hard to lose weight.

What should an Endomorph Eat?

If you are an endomorph and you are interested in losing weight as well as have some muscle definition, you may need to look out for a fitness plan and a diet that suits your exact body type.

From the diet's theory, it is seen that endomorphic people have slower metabolisms. This means that they don't burn calories as fast as people in the mesomorph and the ectomorph somatotype. The excess calories stored in the body of endomorphs end up converting to fat.

There is also the belief that individuals in this class have less tolerance for carbohydrates. Due to this, the best diet plan for your body type would be one that has a higher intake of protein and fat and a lower intake of carbohydrates like the paleo diet.

This diet would not only help you lose some body fats but would also keep up your energy level. Good sources of proteins and fats are:
- Cheese
- Olive oil
- Macadamia nuts
- Beef
- Fatty fish
- Egg yolk
- Walnuts

However, this does not mean that you should totally cut off carbs from your diet as they are a great source of energy. People who cut off carb from their diet tend to experience fatigue and sluggishness. If you go too low on the low-carb diet, it may result in ketosis and gastrointestinal problems.

The solution to this is to go for the right type of carbs. Concentrate on complex carbs like vegetables, legumes, tubers, fruits, whole grains, and starchy vegetables like potatoes.

Lower your intake of simple carbohydrates as they contain lots of calories and sugar and can lead to fat storage in an endomorph body. Examples of simple carbohydrates are pasta, white bread, cakes, white rice, and cookies.

Fruits are another healthy addition to any diet plan. You can eat the fruits in moderation if you are sensitive to carbs.

The American Council of Exercise has advised that you follow the formula below when planning your daily meals:

- 35 percent protein
- 30 percent carbohydrates
- 35 percent fat

It is also important that you control the portion of food you consume when trying to reduce body fat as an endomorph, to avoid consuming excess calories. Reducing your calorie consumption by about 200 to 500 will go a long way in helping you to achieve your weight loss goals.

According to the supporters of this diet, endomorphs are not able to lose weight by dieting alone as endomorphs are not quick to drop body fats. As an endomorph, you also need to exercise regularly. You need to include physical activities in your daily routine. This advice isn't just for endomorphs alone, as physical activities help one to be healthy and strong. Not only that, carrying out physical activities every day will help to keep sicknesses away from you.

To achieve a good result with your fitness plan, you need to combine cardio training with weight training.

Diet and Weight Loss

Because endomorphs are sensitive to insulin and carbohydrates, the best nutrition diet should focus on the equal distribution of macronutrients. A larger percentage of carbohydrates should come from vegetables and a small amount of unrefined, high fiber starches like amaranth and quinoa.

Avoid the cereal, cookie, bread, and cracker aisles in that supermarket! The best diet for an endomorph is the paleo-like diet, which contains vegetables, proteins, and some healthy fats like olive oil and avocado. Let your aim be for a nutrient distribution that has at least 35% protein, 30% carbs, and 35% fat.

Best Choice for Breakfast

Start your day with a breakfast rich in protein to help jumpstart the metabolism and prevent the insulin levels from going high. My favorite choice for endomorphs breakfast is the omelet or Pomodoro frittata. Find the recipe below:

Pomodoro Frittata

Serving: 4

Total time: 35 min

Ingredients:

- Nonfat milk - ½ cup
- Basil - - ½ cup
- Three eggs and three egg whites
- Three cloves of garlic
- 3 Roma tomatoes
- ¼ cup of fresh Parmesan cheese

Instructions

1. Break the eggs in a small bowl and whisk together.
2. Remove the seed from the tomatoes then chop. Slice the basil thin. Mince the garlic.
3. Heat your oven to 350 degrees F. Apply olive oil cooking spray on a glass pie plate.
4. Whisk all your ingredients together in a big bowl. Pour the mixture into the pie plate.
5. Place in your oven and allow to bake for 25 minutes or until the eggs are done.
6. Take out of the oven, allow the steam to cool before you slice into wedges.

Chapter 3: Fitness Goals

Because it's difficult for an endomorph to lose fat by just dieting, you have to also have a well-rounded fitness program. Exercise will help to boost your metabolism, especially when it's a combination of cardio and weight training. This is to say that you have to dedicate yourself to a lifelong program without overdoing it.

While it's easy for an endomorph to build muscles, it is much harder to stay lean due to the slow metabolism and the excess body fat.

To start, try out several activities until you find out the one that does not get you easily bored and will not make you overtrain. Let us look at the activities below:

Cardio

Although it is advised to relax and take it easy with your training, you must, however, keep yourself in motion, like every day, to resist the urge to chill out. Cardio training is important as it allows the endomorph to burn calories and create a large deficit for calories.

Recommendations for Cardio Training for Endomorphs

Carry out a High-intensity Interval Training (HIIT) at least 2 to 3 days in a week for a maximum of 30 minutes for each workout.

Also, include a 30 to 60 minutes steady-state cardio training every 2 to 3 days a week.

Explaining High-Intensity Interval Training (HIIT),
Several people think that cardio training is just to take long but boring jogs on the treadmill or even pedaling an upright bike for an extended time. However, cardio training is all about high-intensity interval training (HIIT), which interchanges between the very high-intensity exercise rounds and either a complete rest or a low-intensity round of exercise. This is different from the 30 to 60 minutes of ongoing steady-

state cardio that the majority do on the cardio machines.

HIIT workouts are done in lesser time than the old cardio workout but achieve the same if not better results. Benefits of doing the HIIT workouts are:

- It raises your metabolic rate to help burn extra calories while exercising and resting.
- It increases the anaerobic and aerobic pathways that help to utilize and take in more oxygen during steady-state training.
- It also helps you to carry out the anaerobic exercises for a longer time.
- It helps you to break through training tables.
- Increase in EPOC (excess post-exercise oxygen consumption), which leads to a longer and higher burning of calories even after you have stopped the exercise.

You can do the HIIT workouts on any cardio machine that can vary speed or resistance.

Treadmills allow you to grow your speed and incline, which makes it a good choice for cardio exercises. Bikes allow you to grow both your speed and your resistance.

The elliptical trainer, on the other hand, has additional features that you can use to increase speed, resistance, and ramp height. If you can get the elliptical trainer that comes with arm handles, you will be able to include your upper body in the exercise. If you can finish a minimum of 30 minutes of cardiovascular activity of low to moderate speed on any cardio machines, then you are ready to begin HIIT workouts using the elliptical trainer.

Warm-Up:

The first 5 minutes you spend on the elliptical trainer should be to concentrate on getting your body ready for the workout. Use 5 minutes to pedal from a low to a moderate pace just to increase body temperature as well as get the body ready for more serious work. Spend another

3 minutes playing around with increasing the machine's resistance level, speed, ramp height, or even a combination of all these features to discover your maximum best.

Workout:

The workout involves alternating rounds of low and high intensities for the advised period. The intense short work phase should be the highest level that you can go. While on the longer, low-intensity recovery phase, reduce the resistance, speed, and ramp height to a pace that is okay for you to catch your breath.

Workout #1: For Beginner HIIT

Duration: 23 minutes

Warm-up:	
5 minutes of low to moderate intensity	
3 minutes to explore speed, resistance level, and ramp height to find your maximum best	
Work	**Rest**
30 secs	2 minutes

30 secs	2 minutes
30 secs	1:30 minutes
30 secs	1 minute
30 secs	1:30 minutes
30 secs	2 minutes
30 secs	2 minutes
Cool down: 3 minutes	

As you improve your fitness level and can get back faster than the suggested time above, then you can reduce the time you spend resting.

Workout #2: Intermediate HIIT

Duration: 20 minutes

Warm-up	
5 minutes of moderate-intensity to explore speed, resistance level, and ramp height to find your maximum best	
Work	**Rest**
30 secs	1:30 minutes
30 secs	1:15 minutes

30 secs	1:00 minute
30 secs	1 minute
30 secs	45 seconds
30 secs	45 seconds
30 secs	1 minute
30 secs	1 minute
30 secs	1:30 minutes
30 secs	
Cool down 3 minutes	

Cool down:

Reduce the speed, resistance level, and ramp height a little below the low-intensity settings. Concentrate on reducing your heart rate as well as slowing down your breathing before you get off the machine.

Weight Training

Your focus during weight training sessions should be to maintain or build lean muscle mass, loss some body fat, and increase metabolism. When you develop more active muscle tissue, it helps to increase the resting metabolic rate, which will encourage your body to use up the stored-up fats for fuel.

Recommendations for Weight Training
- Concentrate on the large muscle groups (e.g., back and legs) and high repetitions (15 reps)
- Compound exercises
- Carry out circuit training with minimal rest time between each set.

Circuit Training Workout Guide

Exercise	Time
Squat with overhead press	Workout for 50 sec
Rest	Rest for 10 sec
Stationary lunge with lateral raise (right leg front)	Workout for 50 sec

Rest	Rest for 10 sec
Stationary lunge with lateral raise (left leg front holding dumbbells)	Workout for 50 sec
Rest	Rest for 10 sec
Plié squat/upright row (kettlebell or dumbbells)	Workout for 50 sec
Rest	Rest for 10 sec
Push-ups using a single leg knee to drive	Workout for 50 sec
Rest	Rest for 10 sec
Plank with triceps extension (dumbbells)	Workout for 50 sec
Rest	Rest for 10 sec
Alternate step-ups with hammer curls (dumbbells)	Workout for 50 sec
Repeat three times	

Other Factors to Consider

- Reduce how much time you spend watching TV.
- Reduce your sleep time, rise early.
- Get another person involved in your workouts, a partner, a hired training, or enter a competition

When you are consistent and diligent with your exercise and eating habits, it will help a great deal in your weight loss goal.

Chapter 4

The Beginner's Guide to Paleo Diet

The paleo diet is created to look like what the ancestors (human hunter-gatherer) ate thousands of years ago. Although we cannot exactly say what those human ancestors ate in all the parts of the world, researchers have made us believe that their diets were mainly on whole meals.

It is believed that these hunter-gatherers had a very low rate of lifestyle diseases like diabetes, obesity, and heart disease because of the whole food diets they practiced along with their active lifestyle.

Different studies have also proven that this diet can cause tremendous weight loss without the stress of counting calories. Apart from weight loss, the diet can cause a great improvement in one's health.

Here, I would introduce you to the paleo diet, amazing recipes to try, as well as a sample meal plan to guide your dieting.

Setting Up A Paleo Diet Meal Plan

There is no particular right way for everyone to eat because these paleolithic persons survived on different diets, depending on what they had available and where they were living. While some ate a low carb diet high in animal foods, others did a high carb diet with plenty of plants.

See this as a general guide that you can modify to suit your personal needs and desires. These are the basics:

Food to eat: Fish, meat, eggs, fruits, vegetables, nuts, herbs, seeds, spices, oils, and healthy fats.

What not to eat: Processed foods, soft drinks, sugar, most dairy products, grains, artificial sweeteners, legumes, margarine, vegetable oils, and trans fats.

Foods to Avoid on the Paleo Diet

You should avoid the foods and ingredients below:

- **Corn syrup with high fructose and sugar:** fruit juices, soft drinks, table sugar, pastries candy, ice cream, and many others.
- **Legumes:** lentils, beans, and many more.
- **Grains:** wheat, bread, barley, and pasta, rye, spelt, etc.
- **Dairy:** almost all dairy should be avoided, especially the low fat. (some versions of paleo have the full-fat dairy included in their diet, like cheese and butter)
- **Trans fats:** these are seen in margarine and other processed foods, popularly known as Usually "hydrogenated" or "partially hydrogenated" oils.

- **Some vegetable oils:** sunflower oil, Soybean oil, cottonseed oil, grapeseed oil, corn oil, safflower oil, and others.
- **Artificial sweeteners:** sucralose, aspartame, cyclamates, acesulfame potassium. Natural sweeteners are better.
- **Highly processed foods:** every food labeled as "diet" or "low-fat," as well as foods that contain many additives, including artificial meal replacements.

In summary: do not eat anything that looks like it was manufactured in a factory. To avoid these ingredients, always go through the labels or list on ingredients, even for those foods reads as "health foods."

Foods to Eat on the Paleo Diet

Let your diet focus on whole and unprocessed Paleo foods like:

- **Meat:** lamb, beef, chicken, pork, turkey, and others.
- **Fish and seafood:** shellfish, salmon, haddock, trout, shrimp, etc.
- **Eggs:** Choose omega-3 enriched eggs or pastured, free-range eggs.
- **Fruits:** bananas, Apples, oranges, avocados, pears, blueberries, strawberries, and more.
- **Vegetables:** tomatoes, broccoli, peppers, kale, carrots, onions, etc.
- **Nuts and seeds:** macadamia nuts, almonds, hazelnuts, walnuts, pumpkin seeds, sunflower seeds, and more.
- **Tubers:** Potatoes, yams, sweet potatoes, turnips, etc.
- **Salt and spices:** rosemary, sea salt, turmeric, garlic, etc.
- **Healthy oils and fats:** coconut, extra virgin olive, avocado oil, and others.

It is better to go for organic, pasture-raised, and grass-fed if you can afford it. Otherwise, always go for the option that is the least processed.

Modified Paleo Diets

Over the course of the past few years, there have been so many changes in the paleo community. We now have a variety of paleo diet options. Some of these new diets have added some new foods that are suggested as being healthy by science.

Examples are the grass-fed butter and gluten-free grains like rice. Several people now see the paleo diet as a guide for developing their own diet and not a strict rule that must be followed.

Sensible Indulgences

The beverages and foods listed below can be eaten in moderate quantities:

- **Dark chocolate:** go for the ones that have a minimum of 70% cocoa. If you get the good dark chocolate, they are very healthy and nutritious.
- **Wine:** A very good red wine is rich in antioxidants and has several important nutrients.

What to Drink When You're Thirsty

When it comes to liquid, water should be your best bet.

The drinks listed below are not particularly paleo, but several people on this diet still take them:

- **Coffee:** coffee has a high content of antioxidants and has several health benefits.
- **Tea:** Tea is another liquid that is not only healthy but comes with several benefiting

compounds. The best option for tea is Green tea.

A Paleo Menu Plan for One Week

This meal plan below has a balanced amount of foods that are paleo-friendly. Remember that this serves as a guide, and you can adjust to suit your needs and preferences.

Monday

- **Breakfast:** Eggs with vegetables fried in coconut oil. One fruit.
- **Lunch:** Chicken salad mixed with olive oil. A few nuts.
- **Dinner:** Burgers fried in butter, with some salsa and vegetables.

Tuesday

- **Breakfast:** Eggs and Bacon with one fruit.

- **Lunch:** Eat the burgers remaining from the previous night.
- **Dinner:** Salmon fried in butter, with vegetables.

Wednesday

- **Breakfast:** Meat with leftover vegetables from the previous night.
- **Lunch:** Sandwich wrapped in a lettuce leaf with fresh vegetables and meat.
- **Dinner:** Stir-fry ground beef with vegetables. Add some berries.

Thursday

- **Breakfast:** Boiled eggs with a piece of your choice of fruit.
- **Lunch:** use the grounded beef remaining from the previous night and a handful of nuts.
- **Dinner:** Fried vegetables and pork.

Friday

- **Breakfast:** Fried eggs and vegetables done with coconut oil.
- **Lunch:** Chicken salad mixed with olive oil. A few nuts.
- **Dinner:** Steak with sweet potatoes and vegetables.

Saturday

- **Breakfast:** Eggs and bacon with a piece of any preferred fruit.
- **Lunch:** Steak and vegetables remaining from the previous night.
- **Dinner:** Bake a salmon with avocado and vegetables.

Sunday

- **Breakfast:** Meat with leftover vegetables from the previous night.
- **Lunch:** Sandwich wrapped in a lettuce leaf, with fresh vegetables and meat.
- **Dinner:** Grill some chicken wings with salsa and vegetables.

You do not need to track either calories or macronutrients (carbs, proteins, or fat) while on the paleo diet, at least not when you first start.

However, if your goal is to shed some weight, then you may need to cut down on carbs and reduce how you consume high-fat foods like nuts.

Simple Paleo Snacks

While on the paleo diet, you may necessarily not need to eat more than three meals daily, but if peradventure you get hungry, you can snack on any of the following:

- Hard-boiled eggs
- Baby carrots
- Some nuts
- One fruit
- Slices of Apple with almond butter
- Leftovers from the previous night

- Homemade beef jerky
- A bowl of berries with some coconut cream

Paleo Diet Shopping List

The paleo diet affords you a tremendous variety of food you can eat.

I have written this to help you when shopping:

- **Poultry:** Turkey, Chicken, etc.
- **Meat:** Lamb, beef, pork, etc.
- **Eggs**
- **Fish:** Trout, salmon, mackerel, etc.
- **Frozen vegetables:** Spinach, broccoli, different mixtures of vegetables, etc.
- **Fresh vegetables:** Lettuce, greens, tomatoes, carrots, peppers, onions, etc.
- **Fruits:** bananas, apples, pears, avocado, oranges

- **Nuts:** hazelnuts, walnuts, almonds, macadamia nuts
- **Berries:** blueberries, strawberries, etc.
- **Almond butter**
- **Olive oil**
- **Coconut oil**
- **Sweet potatoes**
- **Olives**
- **Condiments:** pepper, Sea salt, garlic, turmeric, parsley, etc.

It is advisable to remove every unhealthy temptation from your kitchen. This includes pastries, sugary sodas, cookies, bread, crackers, cereals, and ice cream.

How to Make Restaurant Meals Paleo-Friendly

If you have to eat out in restaurants, it is quite easy to order for paleo-friendly meals.

- Let your main dish contain meat or fish.

- Take plain water instead of fruit juice or sugary soda.
- Request for more vegetables as against potatoes, bread, or rice.
- Ask them to prepare your meal using coconut oil or olive oil.

My Favorite Paleo Recipes

The recipes below are part of my favorite. These are recipes that you can make at home with ingredients that are available in the stores.

Broiled Salmon

Serves 4

Prep time: 10 min

Total time: 20 min

Ingredients
- Grainy mustard - 1 tablespoon
- Salmon - 4 (4-oz.) fillets
- Garlic - 2 cloves (finely minced)

- Fresh thyme leaves, chopped, - 2 teaspoons (plus more for garnish)
- Finely minced shallots - 1 tablespoon
- Fresh rosemary, chopped - 2 teaspoons
- Juice of half a lemon
- Freshly ground black pepper
- Kosher salt
- Lemon slices, for serving

Instructions

1. Heat the broiler. Line parchment paper on a baking sheet
2. Mix the shallot, garlic, mustard, lemon juice, rosemary, and thyme in a bowl. Season with salt and pepper. Spread the mixture all over the salmon fillets, then place the salmon in the broiler and broil for about 7 to 8 minutes.
3. Take out of the broiler, garnish with more lemon slices and thyme. Serve!

Paleo Chili

Serves 6

Prep time: 15 min

Total time: 55 min

Ingredients

- Lean ground beef - 2 lb.
- Bacon - 3 slices (cut into ½" strips)
- Celery stalks - 2 (chopped)
- Medium yellow onion – ½ (chopped)
- Bell peppers - 2 (chopped)
- Garlic - 3 cloves (minced)
- Dried oregano - 2 teaspoons
- Chili powder - 2 tablespoons
- Ground cumin - 2 teaspoons
- Fire-roasted tomatoes - 1 (28-oz.) Can
- Smoked paprika - 2 tablespoons
- Low-sodium chicken broth - 2 cups
- Freshly ground black pepper
- Kosher salt
- Sliced jalapeños, for garnish
- Freshly chopped cilantro, for garnish

- Sliced avocado, for garnish

Instructions

1. Cook the bacon in a large pot over medium heat. Remove the bacon from the pot once it turns crisp. Then add the celery, onion, and peppers to the pot and cook for approximately 6 minutes, until soft. Then add the garlic and cook for another one minute, until fragrant.
2. Push the cooked veggies to one side of the pot and add the beef. Cook the beef until there is no pink side remaining, stirring occasionally. Drain fat and return to heat.
3. Add the paprika, chili powder, oregano, and cumin to the pot, then season with salt and pepper. Stir the content of the pot thoroughly, then cook for another two minutes. Add the chicken broth and tomatoes and allow to simmer. Then cook

for another 10 to 15 minutes, until the chili is slightly thickened.

4. Serve into bowls, then add the reserved bacon, avocado, cilantro, and jalapeños on top.

Easy Paleo Meatball

Serves 6

Prep time: 15 min

Total time: 1 hour 15 min

Ingredients

- Extra-virgin olive oil - 2 tablespoons
- Garlic - 3 cloves, minced
- Small onion - 1, finely chopped
- Dried oregano - 1 teaspoon
- Kosher salt
- Mustard powder - ¼ teaspoon
- Ground beef - 2 lb.
- Coconut aminos - 2 tablespoons (divided)
- Almond flour - ½ cups
- Large eggs – 2

- Tomato paste - ¼ cup
- Garlic powder - ½ teaspoon
- Apple cider vinegar - 2 tablespoons
- A pinch of cayenne pepper
- Freshly ground black pepper
- Cooking spray

Instructions

1. Heat your oven to 350 degrees F. Place parchment paper on a loaf pan and grease with cooking spray.
2. Place a large skillet over medium heat, add two tablespoons of oil and heat. Add the garlic and onion, cook for about 5 minutes, until soft. Season with pepper, salt, and oregano. Set aside to cool.
3. Mix the beef, one tablespoon of coconut aminos, eggs, almond flour, and the onion mixture in a large bowl – season with salt and pepper. Press the beef mixture into the greased loaf pan.

4. Add the remaining coconut aminos, the vinegar, tomato paste, mustard powder, garlic powder, and the cayenne into a medium bowl – season with salt and pepper.
5. Brush the vinegar mixture all over the meatloaf.
6. Place the pan in the oven to bake for about one hour until well cooked, and the internal temperature reaches 155 degrees F.
7. Set the pan aside to cool for about 15 minutes before you serve.

Perfect paleo pizza

Serves 4

Prep time: 10 min

Total time: 30 min

Ingredients

- Almond flour - 2 ½ cups (plus more for dusting)
- Italian seasoning - 1 teaspoon
- Baking powder - ½ teaspoon
- Small green bell pepper - ½ (thinly sliced)
- Cremini mushrooms - 2 (thinly sliced)
- Large pinch garlic powder
- Sliced black olives - ¼ cup
- Large eggs - 3
- Small red onion - ¼ (thinly sliced)
- Extra-virgin olive oil - 2 tablespoons
- Shredded dairy-free mozzarella - 1 cup
- Pizza sauce - ½ cup
- Pepperoni slices - ¼ cup
- Kosher salt - ½ teaspoon
- Pinch red pepper flakes

Instructions
1. Heat your oven to 425 degrees F, with a rack in the top third.

2. Mix the baking powder, garlic powder, Italian seasoning, almond flour, and salt in a large bowl.
3. Break the eggs into a small bowl, add the olive oil and whisk together. Now pour this mixture into the bowl with the dry ingredients. Stir thoroughly until a dough forms.
4. Place a piece of parchment paper on a surface, transfer the dough to the parchment paper, then place another piece of parchment paper on top. Roll out the dough into ¼-inch thickness. Dispose of the top parchment paper.
5. Slide the bottom parchment paper into a baking sheet, with a crust. Bake for about ten minutes, until the crust is lightly golden.
6. Spread the pizza sauce over the dough, leaving a half-inch border.

7. Top with the mozzarella and the vegetable toppings, then return the pan to the oven and bake for another ten minutes, until the crust is golden and the cheese is melted.
8. Set the oven to broil and broil for about two minutes until the cheese is golden.
9. Garnish with the red pepper flakes before you serve.

Baked Garlic-Butter Salmon

Serves 4

Prep time: 10 min

Total time: 25 min

Ingredients
- One large salmon fillet (about 3 lb.)
- Two lemons, thinly sliced
- Chopped thyme leaves - 1 teaspoon
- Chopped fresh parsley, for garnish
- Honey - 2 tablespoons

- Freshly ground black pepper
- Butter - 6 tablespoons (melted)
- Garlic - 3 cloves (minced)
- Kosher salt
- Dried oregano - 1 teaspoon

Instructions

1. Heat your oven to 350 degrees F. Line a rimmed baking sheet with foil, then spray with cooking spray. Lay the lemon slices in the center of the foil in an even layer.
2. Season all the sides of the salmon with salt and pepper, then place the salmon on top of the lemon slices.
3. Mix the butter, oregano, thyme, garlic, and honey in a bowl. Pour the mixture over the salmon, then fold up the foil around the salmon.
4. Place the salmon in the oven to bake for about 25 minutes, until well cooked. Set the oven to broil and broil for

approximately two minutes, or until the butter mixture turns thick.

5. Take out of the oven, garnish with parsley before you serve.

Paleo Bread

Serves 6

Prep time: 10 min

Total time: 45 min

Ingredients

- Coconut flour - 2 tablespoons
- Flaxseed meal - 2 tablespoons
- Apple cider vinegar - 1 tablespoon
- Almond flour - 1 2/3 cup
- Baking soda - 2 teaspoons
- Kosher salt - ½ teaspoon
- Extra-virgin olive oil - ¼ cup
- Large eggs - 5
- Agave syrup - 1 tablespoon

Instructions

1. Heat your oven to 350 degrees F. Place parchment paper on an 8-inch by 5-inch loaf pan.
2. Mix the flaxseed meal, baking soda, salt, coconut flour, and almond flour in a large bowl. Then add the agave, apple cider vinegar, olive oil, and eggs. Whisk together until completely combined and smooth.
3. Transfer the batter to the greased pan, smoothen the top with a spatula.
4. Place the pan in the oven to bake for approximately 35 minutes, or until the top turns golden, and a toothpick inserted into the center of the batter comes out clean.
5. Lift the loaf out of the pan and allow it to cool completely before you slice.

Whole 30 Chicken Cacciatore

Serves 4

Prep time: 30 min

Total time: 1 hour 20 min

Ingredients

- Mushrooms - 1 cup (sliced)
- Onion - ½ (minced)
- Capers - 1 tablespoon (drained)
- Garlic - 2 cloves (minced)
- Cooking fat - 4 tablespoons
- Chicken thighs - ½ lb.
- Bone-in skin-on chicken legs - 1 lb.
- Kosher salt - ½ teaspoon
- Chicken broth or water - 1 cup
- Red bell pepper - ½ (finely chopped)
- Diced tomatoes - 1 (14.5-oz.) Can
- Freshly ground black pepper - ½ teaspoon
- Fresh basil leaves, roughly chopped - 1 tablespoon

Instructions

1. Heat two tablespoons of cooking fat in a large skillet with high edges, over

medium-high heat, swirling to coat the bottom of the skillet. Thoroughly season the chicken with pepper and salt, then place the chicken in the pan. Sear the chicken for about 3 minutes on each side until golden brown.

2. Take out the chicken from the skillet and keep aside. Add the remaining cooking fat into the skillet, add the onions, and peppers and sauté for about three minutes, until the onion becomes transparent.

3. Add the mushroom to the pan and cook for two minutes, stirring occasionally. Add the garlic, and stir for about one minute, then add the diced tomatoes and capers.

4. Place the chicken back into the pan, then pour in the water or chicken broth, enough to cover the content of the pan. Reduce your heat to medium and allow everything to simmer.

5. Then further reduce the heat to low and continue to simmer for about thirty minutes, until the chicken reaches an internal temperature of 160 degrees F.

BLT Burgers

Serves 4

Prep time: 25 min

Cook time: 35 min

Ingredients

- Tomatoes – 2 (sliced)
- Juice of ½ lemon
- Butterhead lettuce, for serving
- Bacon slices - 1 lb. (halved)
- Finely chopped chives - 3 tablespoon
- Kosher salt
- Ground beef - 1 lb.
- Mayonnaise - ½ cup
- Fresh ground black pepper

Instructions

1. Heat your oven to 400 degrees F. Place a baking rack inside of a baking sheet to catch oil.
2. Prepare the bacon weave: line three bacon halves on a baking rack, side by side. Lift one end of the bacon slice in the middle, and place a fourth bacon half on top of the two slices by the side and under the slice in the center. Then lay the middle slice back on the rack.
3. Now lift the two bacon slices by the side and place a fifth bacon half on top of the middle piece and underneath the two slices by the side. Then lay the slices back down.
4. Next, lift the other end of the slice in the middle, and place the 6th slice of bacon on top of the sides pieces and underneath the slice in the middle. Repeat to make a second bacon weave.

5. Season the bacon with pepper and bake in the oven for 25 minutes, until the bacon is crispy. Transfer the bacon slices to a plate lined with a paper towel and allow it to cool for about ten minutes.
6. Prepare your burgers: heat your grill or grill pan to medium-high heat. Shape the ground beef into large patties and season all the sides with pepper and salt. Grill the ground beef for about four minutes on each side, until well cooked to your taste.
7. Make your herb mayo: mix the mayonnaise, chives, and lemon juice in a small bowl.
8. Assemble the burgers: place a bacon wave on the bottom of each burger, then spread some herb mayo on top, top with the burger, tomato, lettuce, and the remaining bacon weave. Serve.

Baked Swordfish Steak

Serves 4

Prep time: 10 min

Total time: 30 min

Ingredients

- Juice of half a lemon
- Freshly ground black pepper
- Extra-virgin olive oil - 3 tablespoons (divided)
- Finely chopped red onion - ¼ cup
- Swordfish steaks – 3
- Kosher salt
- Multicolored cherry tomatoes, halved - 2 pt.
- Thinly sliced basil - 3 tablespoon

Instructions

1. Heat oven to 400 degrees F.
2. Add two tablespoons of olive oil into a large cast-iron skillet over high heat. Once

the oil is heated, add the fish and season the top side with pepper and salt. Cook the fish for about 4 to 5 minutes on one side, until the fish turns brown. Then flip and season the other side with pepper and salt. Cook for another three minutes, until brown. Then put off heat and place the pan in the oven to roast for about ten minutes, until the fish is flaky and well cooked.

3. Prepare your tomato salad: mix the tomatoes, basil, and onion in a large bowl. Add the lemon juice and one tablespoon of olive oil into the bowl, stir together and season with salt and pepper.

4. Spread the salad over the roasted fish and serve.

Lemony Grilled Salmon

Serves 4

Prep time: 10 min

Total time: 20 min

Ingredients

- 4 (6-oz.) skin-on salmon fillets
- Freshly ground black pepper
- kosher salt
- Two tablespoons of butter
- Two lemons, sliced
- Extra-virgin olive oil, for brushing

Instructions

1. Heat the grill to high. Brush the salmon fillets with the olive oil and season with pepper and salt.
2. Place the lemon slices and the salmon to your grill and grill for approximately five minutes on each side, until the lemons are charred and the salmon is well cooked.
3. Take out the salmon from the grill and place the butter on the salmon immediately, then top with the grilled lemons.

Sweet Potato Chili (Paleo-Friendly)

Serves 6

Prep time: 15 min

Total time: 50 min

Ingredients

- Freshly ground black pepper
- Large sweet potatoes - 4 (peeled and cubed into 1-inch pieces)
- Diced tomatoes - 1 (14.5-oz.) Can
- Medium onion – 1 (chopped)
- Extra-virgin olive oil - 2 tablespoons
- Bell pepper – 1 (chopped)
- Tomato paste - 1 tablespoon
- Low-sodium chicken broth - 3 cup
- Garlic - 3 cloves (minced)
- Italian sausage - 1 lb.
- Dried oregano - 1 teaspoon
- Chili powder - 1 tablespoon
- Garlic powder - ½ teaspoon
- Cayenne - ¼ teaspoon

- Kosher salt
- Freshly chopped parsley, for serving

Instructions

1. Heat the oil in a large pot over medium heat. Add the bell pepper and chopped onion and cook for approximately five minutes, until soft. Add the garlic and cook for another one minute, until fragrant. Then add the tomato paste and stir until the content of the pot is well coated. Add the sausage and cook for 7 minutes, stirring with a wooden spoon to break up the meat, until no longer pink. Add the garlic powder, cayenne, oregano, and chili powder – season with salt and pepper.

2. Add the chicken broth, tomatoes, and sweet potatoes and allow to boil. Reduce the heat, cover the pot, and allow to simmer for about 15 minutes, until the sweet potatoes are tender.

3. Garnish with parsley before you serve.

Slow-cooker Paleo Meatballs

Yields 24 meatball

Prep time: 15 min

Total time: 5 hours 45 min

Ingredients

For the Meatballs

- Ground beef - 1 ½ lb.
- Crushed red pepper flakes - ½ teaspoon
- Freshly chopped parsley - ¼ cup (plus more for garnish)
- Large egg – 1
- Kosher salt - 1 teaspoon
- Garlic – 2 cloves, minced

For the Sauce

- Tomato paste - 1 (6-oz.) Can
- Crushed tomatoes - 1 (28-oz.) Can
- Yellow onion - ¼ (finely chopped)
- Garlic – 1 clove, minced

- Dried oregano - 2 teaspoons
- Freshly ground black pepper
- Kosher salt

Instructions

1. Prepare the meatballs: mix the beef, egg, garlic, parsley, red pepper flakes, and salt in a large bowl until well combined. From the mixture, make 24 meatballs and place in the slow cooker.
2. Make your sauce: mix the tomato paste, oregano, garlic, onion and crushed tomatoes, season with salt and pepper, then pour the mixture over the meatballs
3. Cover the slow cooker and cook on low heat for about five and a half hours, until the meatballs are well cooked.
4. Garnish with parsley before you serve.

Paleo Breakfast Stacks

Serves 3

Prep time: 10 min

Total time: 30 min

Ingredients

- Avocado – 1, mashed
- Breakfast sausage patties – 3
- Freshly ground black pepper
- Kosher salt
- Large eggs – 3
- Hot sauce, if desired
- Chives, for garnish

Instructions

1. Heat the breakfast sausage according to the instruction on the package.
2. Spray a medium skillet with cooking spray and place over medium heat. Also, spray the inside of a mason jar lid with cooking spray. Place the mason jar lid in the middle of the pot, then break the eggs inside the jar lid. Season with salt and pepper, then cook for approximately three minutes, until all the whites are set, then take out

the lid and continue to cook until the eggs are done.

3. Spread the mashed potato on top of the breakfast sausage and season with salt and pepper, then place the egg on top. Garnish with chives and drizzle with your preferred hot sauce.

Bell Pepper Eggs

Serves 3

Prep time: 5 min

Total time: 20 min

Ingredients

- Bell pepper – 1 (sliced into ¼-inch rings)
- Kosher salt
- Eggs - 6
- Freshly ground black peppers
- Chopped parsley - 2 tablespoons
- Chopped chives - 2 tablespoons

Instructions

1. Place a non-stick skillet over medium heat, then lightly spray with cooking spray.
2. Place one bell pepper ring in the skillet, then sauté for approximately two minutes. Turn the ring to the other side, then break one egg into the center of the ring. Season with salt and pepper, cook for about two to four minutes, or until the egg is well cooked.
3. Repeat with the other eggs and pepper rings.
4. Garnish with parsley and chives.

One-Pan Balsamic Chicken and Asparagus

Serves 4

Prep time: 20 min

Total time: 40 min

Ingredients

- Garlic - 2 cloves, minced
- Dijon mustard - 1 tablespoon
- Freshly ground black pepper
- Asparagus - 1 lb., woody ends trimmed
- Extra-virgin olive oil - ¼ cup (divided)
- Balsamic vinegar - ¼ cup
- Honey - 1 tablespoon
- Pinch of crushed red pepper flakes
- Cherry tomatoes - 1 pt. , halved
- Chicken breast tenders - 2 lb.
- Kosher salt

Instructions

1. Make the vinaigrette: mix the honey, two tablespoons of olive oil, the balsamic vinegar, red pepper flakes, garlic, and mustard in a small bowl until well combined. Set aside.
2. Heat the remaining oil in a large skillet over medium heat. Add the chicken to the pot, season with pepper and salt. Sear for about three minutes on each side, until

golden. Remove the chicken from the pan and set aside.

3. Add the tomatoes and asparagus into the skillet, season with pepper and salt, and cook for about five minutes, until the tomatoes are slightly wilted and the asparagus turns bright green.

4. Shift the veggies to one side of the pot, add the chicken to the pot, then pour in the vinaigrette. Toss the chicken and vegetables slightly for another five minutes, until the vinaigrette is thickened and the chicken is cooked through. Serve.

Broccoli Bacon Salad

Serves 4 to 6

Prep time: 15 min

Total time: 25 min

Ingredients

For the Salad

- Bacon – 6 slices, cooked and crumbled
- Sliced almonds - ½ cup
- Red onion - ½, thinly sliced
- Dried cranberries - ½ cup
- Broccoli – 3 heads, cut into bite-size pieces
- Kosher salt
- Carrots – 2, shredded

For the Dressing
- Apple cider vinegar - 3 tablespoons
- Mayonnaise - ½ cup
- Freshly ground black pepper
- kosher salt

Instructions
1. Boil four cups of salted water in a medium saucepan.
2. While the water is heating, prepare a large bowl with ice water and set aside.
3. Add the broccoli to the water once it boils, then cook for about 2 minutes, until tender. Use a slotted spoon to remove the broccoli and place it in the ice water. Once

the veggie is cool, drain the florets in a colander.
4. Mix the carrots, cranberries, bacon, red onion, nuts, and broccoli in a large bowl.
5. Mix the vinegar and mayonnaise in another bowl, season with salt and pepper. Pour this dressing over the broccoli and stir to coat—dish into serving bowls.

Classic Chicken Salad

Serves 8 to 10

Prep time: 10 min

Total time: 25 min

Ingredients
- One green apple, chopped
- Three chicken breasts
- Half red onion, finely chopped
- Mayonnaise - 2/3 cup
- Two celery stalks, finely chopped
- Two tablespoons of lemon juice

- kosher salt
- One tablespoon of chopped dill, for garnish
- Freshly cracked black pepper
- Six sprigs of dill (optional)
- Six slices of lemon (optional)

Instructions

1. Poach the chicken breast: arrange the chicken in a singer layer into a large pot. Place the dill sprigs and lemon slices on the chicken. Pour water into the pot, enough to cover at least an inch of the chicken. Allow the water to boil, then reduce to simmer and cook for approximately ten minutes, or until the center of the chicken gets to 165 degrees F when reading with a thermometer. Alternatively, check that the thickest part of the chicken has turned opaque.
2. Take out the chicken from the pot and cut into bite-size pieces.

3. Mix the chopped chicken, celery, onion, and apple in a large bowl.
4. Mix the lemon juice and mayonnaise in another bowl, season with salt and pepper, and combine.
5. Pour the dressing over the chicken and toss.
6. Garnish with some more dill before you serve.

Tuna Salad Pickle Boats

Serves 6

Prep time: 15 min

Total time: 15 min

Ingredients

- Mayonnaise - ¼ cup
- Tuna - 2 5-oz. cans, drained
- Dijon mustard - 1 tablespoon
- Juice of half a lemon
- Celery - 2 stalks, finely chopped

- Freshly ground black pepper
- Chopped dill - 1 tablespoon, plus more for garnish
- Dill pickles - 6
- Kosher salt
- Paprika, for garnish

Instructions

1. Mix the lemon juice, Dijon, dill, mayonnaise, tuna, and celery in a large bowl. Season with pepper and salt, mix until combined.
2. Slice the pickles in half lengthwise. Use a spoon to scoop out the seeds and form boats. Fill each boat with the tuna mixture, garnish with more dill and paprika.

Breakfast Tomatoes

Serves 3

Prep time: 5 min

Total time: 45 min

Ingredients

- Chives - 1 tablespoon, thinly chopped
- Three large tomatoes
- Freshly ground black pepper
- olive oil - 1 tablespoon
- kosher salt
- Three eggs
- freshly grated Parmesan, for serving

Instructions

1. Heat your oven to 400 degrees F. Line a small baking sheet with parchment paper. Slice off the tops of the tomatoes, then use a metal spoon to scoop the inside of the tomatoes and make a hollow. Drizzle the tomatoes with olive oil and season with pepper and salt.
2. Place the tomatoes on the baking sheet and bake in the oven for approximately 10

minutes until a little bit softened. Break one egg each into the center of each of the tomatoes. Place the tomatoes back into the oven to bake for another 15 minutes, until the egg is cooked as you like it. Season with salt and pepper again to taste, then garnish with Parmesan and chives. Serve.

Brussels Sprouts Hash

Serves 4

Prep time: 10 min

Total time: 40 min

Ingredients

- Bacon - 6 slices, cut into 1-inch pieces
- ½ onion, chopped
- Crushed red pepper flakes - ¼ teaspoon
- 1 lb. of brussels sprouts, trimmed and quartered
- Garlic - 2 cloves, minced

- Four large eggs
- Freshly ground black pepper
- Kosher salt

Instructions

1. Cook the bacon in a large skillet over medium heat until crispy. Put off the heat, then transfer the bacon to a plate lined with a paper towel. Retain the bacon fat in the skillet, use a spoon to remove any black pieces from the pot.
2. Set the heat to medium, then add the Brussel sprouts and the onion to the skillet. Cook until the veggies start to turn soft and golden, stirring occasionally. Season with the red pepper flakes, salt, and pepper.
3. Add two tablespoons of water to the skillet and cover with a lid. Cook for another five minutes, until the water has evaporated and the Brussel sprouts are tender. If the water dries before the

sprouts are tender, add more water to the pot and cook for a few more minutes. Add the garlic to the pot and cook for another one minute, until fragrant.

4. Use a wooden spoon to make four holes in the hash, deep enough to reveal the bottom of the skillet. Break an egg into each hole, then season the eggs with salt and pepper. Cover with a lid and cook for another five minutes, until the eggs are cooked as you like them.
5. Turn off heat, sprinkle the cooked bacon bits over the content of the skillet. Serve warm.

Grilled Chicken Breast

Serves 4

Prep time: 15 min

Total time: 45 min

Ingredients

- Four chicken breasts
- Extra-virgin olive oil - 3 tablespoons
- Balsamic vinegar - ¼ cup
- Brown sugar - 2 tablespoons
- Garlic - 3 cloves, minced
- Dried rosemary - 1 teaspoon
- Dried thyme - 1 teaspoon
- Kosher salt
- Freshly chopped parsley, for garnish
- Freshly ground black pepper

Instructions

- Whisk together the olive oil, balsamic vinegar, dried herbs, garlic, and brown sugar in a large bowl. Season generously with pepper and salt. Take out ¼ cup of the mixture and set aside.
- Add the chicken to the bowl, toss to combine. Keep the bowl aside to marinate for a minimum of 20 minutes or overnight.
- Heat your grill to medium-high. Add the chicken and grill for about six minutes on

each side, basting with the mixture that you reserved, until well cooked.
- Garnish with parsley before you serve.

Paleo Chocolate Chip Cookies

Yields 24 cookies

Prep time: 10 min

Total time: 25 min

Ingredients
- Pure vanilla extract - 1 teaspoon
- Almond flour - 2 cup
- Almond butter - ¼ cup
- Kosher salt - ¼ teaspoon
- Baking soda - ½ teaspoon
- Butter - ¼ cup, room temperature
- Semisweet chocolate chips - 1 cup
- Honey - 3 tablespoon
- Large egg – 1
- Flaky sea salt

Instructions

1. Heat your oven to 350 degrees F. Place parchment paper on a baking sheet.
2. Whisk together the baking soda, almond flour and salt in a large bowl. Add the almond butter, egg, honey, vanilla, and butter. Then use a hand mixer to beat until combined.
3. Fold in the chocolate chips until combined, then place a tablespoon full of the batter into the baking sheet, until you have exhausted the mixture. Sprinkle the cookies with flaky sea salt.
4. Bake in the oven for about 13 to 15 minutes, until golden.

Balsamic Grilled Chicken and Zucchini

Serves 4

Prep time: 10 min

Total time: 35 min

Ingredients

- Tyson Boneless Skinless Chicken Breasts - 1 ½ lb., pounded to half-inch thickness
- Honey - ½ cup
- Balsamic vinegar - ½ cup
- Freshly ground black pepper
- Orange zest - 1 tablespoon
- Two medium green zucchini (about 1 lb.)
- Chopped fresh oregano - 1 teaspoon
- Two medium yellow zucchini (about 1 lb.)
- kosher salt
- Extra-virgin olive oil
- Sea salt, like Maldon

Instructions

1. Add the balsamic vinegar and the honey into a small saucepan over medium heat. Bring to a boil, then reduce the heat and simmer for ten minutes, until slightly thickened. Put off the heat, stir in the oregano and orange zest. Take out ¼ cup of the mixture and keep aside for serving.

2. Trim off the ends of the zucchini. Use a vegetable peeler or mandolin to create long flat noodles. To get this, run the blade against the length of each of the zucchini. Season with salt and set aside.
3. Heat your grill on medium-high, drizzle the chicken breast with olive oil and season with salt and pepper. Place the spiced chicken on the grill and cook for approximately four minutes on each side.
4. Brush the glaze all over the chicken and cook for another three minutes, until lightly charred all over, and the internal temperature gets to 170 degrees F. Transfer the chicken to a clean plate and cover it loosely with foil.
5. Pour water into an 8-quart stockpot, season generously with salt. Once the water starts to boil, add the zucchini and cook for about three minutes, until al dente. Drain.

6. Slice the chicken against the grain and serve over the zucchini noodles. Drizzle the reserved balsamic glaze on top, then sprinkle with sea salt. Serve immediately.

Parmesan-crusted Salmon

Serves 4

Prep time: 5 min

Total time: 20 min

Ingredients

- Broccoli - 1 head, cut into florets
- Chopped parsley - ¼ cup, plus more for garnish
- Grated Parmesan - 1 cup, plus more for garnish
- Dried oregano - 1 teaspoon
- Extra-virgin olive oil
- Salmon – 4 pieces, about 2 lbs
- Kosher salt
- Freshly ground black pepper

Instructions

1. Mix the oregano, parsley, and parmesan cheese in a small bowl.
2. Brush the salmon with the olive oil and season with black pepper and salt. Place a handful of the cheese mixture on top of each piece of salmon; press down lightly.
3. Heat your oven to 425 degrees F. Place a large non-stick pan or cast-iron skillet over medium heat, then gently place two pieces of the salmon with the cheese side down into the pan and sear for about three minutes, until golden. Move the salmon to a plate with the cheese side up. Wipe the pan to get rid of excess cheese, then repeat with the remaining two pieces of salmon.
4. Now place all the pieces of salmon in your skillet with the cheese side up, and bake in the oven for about four minutes, until cooked through.

5. Meanwhile, add the broccoli into a pot of boiling salted water and cook for approximately two minutes.
6. Transfer the salmon into your serving plate, drizzle olive oil on top, then garnish with Parmesan and parsley. Serve immediately with the cooked broccoli.

Foil-Pack Grilled Salmon with Lemony Asparagus

Serves 4

Prep time: 10 min

Total time: 20 min

Ingredients

- Skin-on salmon fillets - 4 of (6-oz.)
- Asparagus spears - 20, trimmed
- Butter - 4 tablespoon, divided
- kosher salt
- Lemons - 2, sliced
- Torn fresh dill, for garnish
- Freshly ground black pepper

Instructions

1. Spread two pieces of foil on a flat surface, then place five asparagus spears on the foil and top with one salmon fillet, two slices of lemon and one tablespoon of butter. Loosely wrap the foil and set aside. Repeat the steps until you have a total of four packets.
2. Heat the grill on high, then place the four foil packets on the grill for about ten minutes, until the asparagus is tender and the salmon is cooked through.
3. Garnish with dill and serve immediately.

Cajun Shrimp Kebabs

Serves 4 to 6

Prep time: 5 min

Total time: 10 min

Ingredients

- Oregano - 1 teaspoon

- Shrimp - 1 lb.
- Kosher salt - 1 teaspoon
- Olive oil - 2 tablespoons
- Cayenne - 1 teaspoon
- Garlic powder - 1 teaspoon
- Paprika - 1 teaspoon
- Onion powder - 1 teaspoon
- Lemons - 2, sliced thinly crosswise

Instructions
1. Heat the grill to medium-high.
2. Prepare the Cajun spice mix: mix the onion powder, paprika, cayenne, garlic powder, oregano, and salt in a small bowl. Stir with a fork to combine the mixture.
3. Add the olive oil into another bowl, add the shrimps and toss. Add the spice mixture and toss again to evenly coat the shrimp. Thread the shrimp and lemon slices one after the other onto metal skewers. You may also use wooden

skewers that were soaked in water for twenty minutes.
4. Grill the skewers for about five minutes until the lemon is charred, and the shrimp is opaque – flip once halfway.

Italian Chicken Skillet

Serves 4

Prep time: 10 min

Total time: 40 min

Ingredients

- Boneless skinless chicken breasts - 1 lb.
- Extra-virgin olive oil - 2 tablespoons
- Freshly torn basil - ¼ cup
- Crushed tomatoes - 1 oz. (14-oz.) Can
- Freshly ground black pepper
- Medium zucchini - 2, sliced into half moons
- Onion - ½, thinly sliced
- Bell peppers - 2, thinly sliced
- Garlic - 2 cloves, minced

- Low-sodium chicken broth - 1 cup
- Dried oregano - ½ teaspoon
- Kosher salt

Instructions

1. Heat the oil in a large skillet, over medium-high heat. Season the chicken with pepper and salt and cook in the pan for about 8 minutes on each side, until well cooked and golden. Move the chicken to a plate.
2. Add the peppers and onion to the skillet and cook for five minutes, until soft. Add the zucchini and cook for another three minutes, until slightly charred, then add the garlic and cook for another one minute, until fragrant.
3. Add the crushed tomatoes and the broth to the skillet, simmer for ten minutes, then place the chicken back to the pot and top with the vegetables and sauce.
4. Garnish with basil before you serve.

Baked Cajun Salmon

Serves 4

Prep time: 10 min

Total time: 30 min

Ingredients

- Salmon - 4 6-oz. Fillets
- Large white onion - ½, thinly sliced
- Freshly ground black pepper
- dried thyme - 1 tablespoon
- One red bell pepper, thinly sliced
- Extra-virgin olive oil - 3 tablespoons
- One orange bell pepper, thinly sliced
- Garlic powder - 2 teaspoons
- Garlic - 3 cloves, thinly sliced
- Cajun seasoning - 1 tablespoon
- kosher salt
- Paprika - 2 teaspoons

Instructions

1. Heat your oven to 400 degrees F. Add the pepper, garlic, and onions into a large

baking sheet, season with pepper and salt and toss with oil.
2. Prepare your seasoning blend: mix the Cajun seasoning, garlic powder, thyme, and paprika in a small bowl.
3. Place the salmon on the baking sheet, then rub the seasoning blend all over the salmon.
4. Bake in the oven for twenty minutes, until the salmon is cooked through, and the vegetables are tender.

Garlic Parmesan Salmon

Serves 6

Prep time: 15 min

Total time: 40 min

Ingredients

- 1 (3-lb.) salmon fillet
- Extra-virgin olive oil - 1 tablespoon

- Finely grated Parmesan - ¼ cup, plus more for serving
- Freshly chopped parsley - 2 tablespoons
- Garlic - 4 cloves, minced
- Freshly ground black pepper
- Kosher salt
- Lemon wedges, for serving

Instructions

1. Heat your oven to 400 degrees F. Line baking sheet with aluminum foil, then apply cooking spray on the sheet.
2. Mix the Parmesan, parsley, and garlic in a small bowl, season with pepper and salt.
3. Move the salmon to the oiled baking sheet and brush the parmesan mixture all over the salmon.
4. Cover with foil and bake in the oven for about 15 to 20 minutes, until the salmon is cooked through.
5. Sprinkle with more parmesan cheese, then serve with lemon wedges.

Peach Balsamic Chicken

Serves 4

Prep time: 5 min

Total time: 30 min

Ingredients

- Boneless skinless chicken breasts - 4
- Large peaches – 4, sliced
- Extra-virgin olive oil - 1 tablespoon
- Freshly ground black pepper
- Kosher salt
- Garlic - 2 cloves, minced
- Torn fresh basil - 1/3 cup
- Shallot – 1, chopped
- Balsamic vinegar - ¼ cup

Instructions

1. Heat the olive oil in a large skillet, over medium heat. Season the chicken with pepper and salt, then place in the skillet to cook for 8 minutes on each side until golden. Transfer the chicken to a plate.

2. Add the shallot and garlic to the skillet and cook for two minutes, add the peaches and cook for another five minutes, until the peaches are softened. Pour in the balsamic vinegar and simmer for two minutes, until slightly reduced, then stir in the basil.
3. Serve the chicken breasts with balsamic peaches.

Cloud Eggs

Serves 4

Prep time: 15 min

Total time: 20 min

Ingredients
- ½ lb. deli ham, chopped
- Freshly grated Parmesan - 1 cup
- Kosher salt
- Freshly chopped chives, for garnish
- Large eggs - 8

- Freshly ground black pepper

Instructions

1. Heat your oven to 450 degrees F. Spray a large baking sheet with cooking spray. Break the eggs in a bowl, then separate the yolks from the whites; put the yolks in a small bowl and the whites in a large bowl. Use a hand mixer or a whisk to beat the egg white for three minutes, until it forms stiff peaks. Gently fold in the ham and parmesan cheese – season with pepper and salt.

2. Use your spoon to scoop eight mounds of egg whites onto the greased baking sheet and indent the centers to form a nest. Place the sheet in the oven to bake for about three minutes, until lightly golden.

3. Bring out of the oven, gently spoon one egg yolk into the center of each nest, then season with pepper and salt and return to

the oven to bake for another three minutes, until the yolks are set.
4. Garnish with chives before you serve.

Pineapple Salsa Grilled Chicken

Serves 4

Prep time: 10 min

Total time: 25 min

Ingredients

- Juice of 4 limes, divided
- Extra-virgin olive oil - ¼ cup, plus more for the grill
- Freshly chopped cilantro - ¼ cup, plus one tablespoon
- Honey - 2 teaspoons
- Boneless skinless chicken breasts - 1 lb.
- Avocado – 1, diced
- Chopped pineapple - 2 cup
- Red onion - ¼, diced
- Kosher salt

- Freshly ground black pepper

Instructions

1. Prepare marinade: whisk together ¼ cup of olive oil, ¼ cup of cilantro, three limes, and honey. Then season with salt.
2. Place the chicken breasts into a large ziplock bag and pour the marinade into the bag. Shake to coat the chicken in the marinade, then place in the refrigerator for a minimum of two hours, or overnight to marinate.
3. When ready to cook, heat your grill to high. Brush the grill with olive oil, then place the chicken on the grill for about eight minutes on each side until cooked and charred.
4. Mix the pineapple, remaining cilantro, remaining lime juice, red onion, and avocado in a bowl—season with pepper and salt.

5. Spoon the mixture over the chicken before you serve.

Whole Roasted Cauliflower, Tomatoes, and Garlic

Serves 4

Prep time: 15 min

Total time: 1 hour 15 min

Ingredients

- Grape or cherry tomatoes – 4 cups
- Chopped fresh flat-leaf parsley - ¼ cup
- Cauliflower - 1 medium head (about 2 ¼ lbs.)
- Extra-virgin olive oil - 4 tablespoons, divided
- Crushed red pepper flakes - ¼ teaspoon
- Kosher salt - ½ teaspoon, divided
- Paprika - 1/8 teaspoon
- Garlic - 4 cloves, peeled and smashed
- Freshly ground black pepper - ¼ teaspoon

Instructions

1. Heat your oven to 400 degrees F with the oven rack in the middle.
2. Place the garlic and tomatoes in a large baking dish, drizzle three tablespoons of olive oil over the tomatoes, then sprinkle with red pepper flakes, pepper, and ¼ teaspoon of salt. Toss to coat.
3. Trim off the large green leaves from the cauliflower, then trim the stem to make the cauliflower sit flat. Push the tomatoes to one side, then add the cauliflower in the middle of the baking dish. Drizzle the remaining olive oil over the cauliflower and rub all over the cauliflower. Sprinkle with the remaining salt and paprika.
4. Roast in the oven for one hour, or until the cauliflower is tender and can be pierced with a paring knife.
5. Take out of the oven and sprinkle parsley over the cauliflower.

6. Cut the cauliflower into wedges and serve with the garlic and tomato mixture.

Cilantro Lime Salmon

Serves 4

Prep time: 15 min

Total time: 35 min

Ingredients

- Extra-virgin olive oil - 2 tablespoons
- Low-sodium vegetable broth - ½ cup
- Salmon - 4 (6-oz.) Fillets
- Freshly ground black pepper
- Butter - 2 tablespoons
- Lime juice - ¼ cup
- Garlic - 2 cloves, minced
- Honey - 2 tablespoons
- Freshly chopped cilantro - ¼ cup, plus more for garnish
- Cumin - ½ teaspoon
- Kosher salt

- Cooked white rice - 1 ½ cup, for serving

Instructions

1. Heat the olive oil in a large skillet over medium-high heat. Season the salmon with pepper and salt, then place it into the skillet with the skin side up. Cook the salmon for about 6 minutes, until deeply golden, then flip to the other side and cook for another two minutes. Move the salmon fillets to a plate.
2. Add the garlic and butter to the skillet and cook until the butter is melted and looks foamy, then stir in the broth, cumin, honey, and lime juice. Bring the mixture to a simmer, then add the cilantro and stir.
3. Reduce the heat to medium, then return the salmon to the pot. Simmer for another three to four minutes, until the salmon is well cooked, and the sauce has reduced.
4. Garnish with more cilantro, if desired, and serve over cooked white rice.

Maple Chicken and Carrots

Serves 1

Prep time: 10 min

Total time: 35 min

Ingredients

- Bone-in skin-on chicken thighs - 4
- Freshly ground black pepper
- Whole-grain mustard - 2 tablespoons
- Large carrots - 3, peeled and sliced into ¼ inch thick rounds
- Extra-virgin olive oil - 2 tablespoons
- Garlic - 3 cloves, minced
- Fresh thyme leaves - 1 tablespoon
- Apple cider vinegar - ¼ cup
- Juice of half a lemon
- Maple syrup - ¼ cup
- Kosher salt

Instructions

1. Heat the oven to 425 degrees F. Season the chicken with pepper and salt.
2. Heat one tablespoon of olive oil in a large oven-safe skillet over medium-high heat. Add the seasoned chicken and sear for about two minutes on each side, then transfer the chicken to a plate.
3. Add the apple cider vinegar to the skillet, use a wooden spoon to scrape up the bottom of the pan. Add the maple syrup, garlic, lemon juice, thyme, and mustard, bring to a simmer. Place the chicken back into the pot and spoon the sauce over the chicken thighs. Turn off heat.
4. Add the carrots into a medium bowl, add the remaining olive oil and toss to coat, then season with pepper and salt. Nestle the coated carrots into the skillet, then place the skillet in the oven to bake for approximately 20 minutes, until the

carrots are tender and the chicken is cooked through.
5. Serve with sauce from the pan.

Lemony Chicken with Brussels Sprouts Slaw

Serves 4

Prep time: 15 min

Total time: 35 min

Ingredients

- Bone-in skin-on chicken breasts - 4
- Extra-virgin olive oil - 5 tablespoons, divided
- Chicken stock - ½ cup
- Freshly ground black pepper
- Small lemon - 1, thinly sliced
- Garlic - 6 cloves, smashed
- Juice of 1 lemon
- Brussels sprouts - 1 lb., thinly sliced
- Fresh rosemary - 6 sprigs
- Freshly grated Parmesan - ¼ cup

- Kosher salt

Instructions

1. Heat your oven to 450 degrees F.
2. Heat two tablespoons of olive oil in a large, ovenproof skillet over medium-high heat. Pat-dry the chicken breasts with paper towels, then generously season them with pepper and salt.
3. Sear the chicken in the skillet with the skin side down for about four to five minutes, until golden. Flip the chicken to the other side, add the rosemary, lemons, and garlic into the oil in the skillet and cook for another three minutes.
4. Pour the chicken stock into the skillet, then place the skillet in the oven to roast for about fifteen to seventeen minutes, or until a meat thermometer reads 165 degrees F internal temperature at the deepest part of the meat. Take the skillet

out of the oven and set aside to cool for five minutes.
5. Whisk together the remaining olive oil and the lemon juice in a small bowl.
6. Toss the lemon vinaigrette, Brussels sprouts, and parmesan cheese in a large bowl, then season with pepper and salt.
7. Serve the chicken breast with roasted lemons, rosemary, garlic, and Brussels sprout slaw.

Rainbow Chicken and Veggies

Serves 5

Prep time: 20 min

Total time: 45 min

Ingredients

- Boneless skinless chicken breasts - 1 lb., cubed
- Cherry tomatoes - 2 cups
- Large broccoli – 1 head, florets removed

- Baby carrots - 3 cups
- Yellow bell peppers – 2, thinly sliced
- Cooked brown rice - - 2 cups
- Small red onions – 2, cut into wedges

For the Marinade
- Juice of two limes
- Freshly ground black pepper
- Extra-virgin olive oil - 1/3 cup
- Freshly chopped cilantro - ¼ cup
- Kosher salt

Instructions
1. Heat your oven to 400 degrees F.
2. Place the chicken, tomatoes, red onion, bell peppers, carrots, and broccoli on two large sheet pans.
3. Prepare the marinade: mix the olive oil, cilantro, and lime juice in a medium bowl, then season with pepper and salt. Stir until combined. Pour the marinade over the chicken and vegetables, then season

with more pepper and salt. Toss until well combined.
4. Place the pans in the oven to bake for approximately 25 minutes, until the chicken is cooked through and the veggies are tender.
5. Divide the cooked rice into five plates and top with the roasted chicken and veggies.

Sheet Pan Garlicky Shrimp and Vegetables

Serves 4

Prep time: 10 min

Total time: 35 min

Ingredients

- Extra-virgin olive oil - ¼ cup, plus more for drizzling
- Chopped fresh parsley - ¼ cup, plus more for garnish
- Garlic - 3 cloves, grated
- Onions - 2, peeled and cut into wedges
- Shrimp - 1 lb., peeled and deveined

- Broccoli - 1 head, cut into florets
- Crushed red pepper flakes - 1 teaspoon
- Kosher salt
- Freshly ground black pepper

Instructions

1. Heat your oven to 400 degrees F.
2. Mix the red pepper flakes, parsley, garlic, and olive oil in a small bowl, then season with pepper and salt. Add the shrimp to the bowl, toss and set aside to marinate.
3. Toss the broccoli and onions on a rimmed half sheet pan, drizzle olive oil on top, and season with pepper and salt. Spread out the veggies in a single layer and roast in the oven for approximately 20 minutes.
4. Pour the shrimp and the marinade over the vegetables and toss together.
5. Spread out in a single layer, then return to the oven to bake for another 5 minutes, until the shrimp is pink and lightly toasted.
6. Serve immediately.

Cauliflower Stuffing

Serves 6

Prep time: 15 min

Total time: 40 min

Ingredients

- Butter - 4 tablespoons
- Freshly chopped rosemary - 2 tablespoons
- Onion – 1, chopped
- Freshly chopped sage - 1 tablespoon (or one teaspoon of ground sage)
- Large carrots – 2, peeled and chopped
- Chicken or low-sodium vegetable broth - ½ cup
- Baby Bella mushrooms - 1 cup (8-oz.) Package, chopped
- Celery – 2 stalks, chopped or thinly sliced
- Freshly chopped parsley - ¼ cup
- Small cauliflower – 1 head, chopped
- Kosher salt

- Freshly ground black pepper

Instructions

1. Melt the butter in a large skillet over medium heat. Add the celery, carrot, and onion and sauté for about 7 to 8 minutes, or until soft.
2. Add the mushrooms and cauliflower to the skillet, season with pepper and salt. Cook for another 8 to 10 minutes, until tender.
3. Add the sage, rosemary, and parsley to the skillet. Stir until combined. Pour over the broth and cook for approximately ten minutes, until the liquid is absorbed.
4. Serve

Low Carb Crepes (gluten-free)

Prep time: 10 min

Total time: 15 min

Ingredients

- ¾ cup of almond milk
- 2 tablespoons of flax meal
- 2 tablespoons of coconut floor
- 2 eggs
- 1 tablespoon of coconut oil
- ¼ cup of hemp seeds
- 1 tablespoon of cinnamon
- ¼ cup of apple juice
- A pinch of salt

Instructions

1. Add all the ingredients into a magic bullet or a blender and blend until you get a smooth texture. Allow the batter to rest for about 2 minutes while you get your non-stick pan ready.
2. Heat the non-stick pan over medium-low heat. Once hot, pour in coconut oil or butter and fry the mixture, fry the first side for about 3 minutes, then turn to the second side and fry for one minute.
3. Allow to cool off before you serve!

Paleo Cinnamon Apple Crisp

Prep time: 15 min

Total time: 1 hour 20 min

Ingredients

- 2 ½ teaspoon of cinnamon
- 7/8 medium-sized organic green apples
- Juice of two lemon or limes (
- ¼ teaspoon of sea salt
- ¾ cup of pecan halves
- Four tablespoons of coconut oil or grass-fed unsalted butter
- ¼ cup of honey
- ¾ cup of walnuts halves
- ½ cup of coconut shreds
- One tablespoon of honey, for topping

Instructions

1. Peel the apples and slice them into bits, then mix with the lime/ lemon extracts, cinnamon, and melted honey.

2. Place the apples in an oval glass baking tray.
3. Beat the butter, nuts, sea salt, coconut shreds, and a tablespoon of honey until they all mix. Use a spoon to spread the topping equally on the apple.
4. Heat your oven on 350 degrees F, then place the baking tray covered with a lid into the oven to bake for approximately 30 minutes.
5. Remove the lid and return to the oven for another 30 minutes.

Instructions for the Whipping Cream
1. Simply whip a cold heavy whipping cream using your electric mixer for approximately 5 minutes to get it stiffened.
2. Serve the cinnamon apple crisp and top with the whipping cream.

Paleo Banana Bread Recipe

Prep time: 15 min

Total time: 45 min

Ingredients

- ¼ cup of flaxseed meal
- 1 teaspoon of baking powder
- 2 cups of almond flour
- 1 teaspoon of baking powder
- 4 overripe bananas
- 2/3 cup of chopped nuts
- 1 teaspoon of vanilla extract
- 4 eggs
- 2 tablespoons of local honey

Instructions

1. Heat the oven to 375 degrees F.
2. Mix all the dry ingredients in a big bowl. Mix the eggs, mashed bananas, vanilla, and honey in another bowl.
3. Dig a small hole into the dry ingredients and pour the wet ingredients into the hole. Mix thoroughly.

4. Grease your baking cups, muffin tins, big loaf pans or mini loaf pans, then fill the pan up to ¾ inches.
5. Put in the oven to bake for about 22 to 25 minutes for the muffin tin while the loaves bake for approximately 30 minutes or until you can insert a toothpick into the bread and it comes out clean.
6. Take out of the oven and keep aside to cool
7. Enjoy your bread with grass-fed butter, or almond butter.

Paleo Pumpkin Bars with Coconut Flour

Prep time: 15 min

Total time: 35 min

Ingredients

- ¼ cup of coconut oil
- 1 teaspoon of baking soda
- 5 eggs
- ½ cup of coconut flour
- 1 cup of pumpkin puree

- ½ teaspoon of cinnamon
- ¼ teaspoon of cloves
- ¼ cup of real maple syrup
- A dash of ginger
- ½ teaspoon of nutmeg
- 1 teaspoon of vanilla (optional)

Instructions

1. Heat your oven to 400 degrees F.
2. Add all the ingredients into your mixer and mix it thoroughly. The batter should be thick at this point
3. Evenly spread it on an 8-by-8 inch pan that has been previously oiled or has parchment paper placed on it.
4. Place the pan in the oven to bake for about 15 to 20 minutes, or until when the top turns slightly brown and the middle is set.
5. Serve!

Honey Graham Cracker Pie Crust

Prep time: 10 min

Total time: 35 min

Ingredients

- 1 egg
- ¼ teaspoon of salt
- ¼ cup of almond flour
- 1 teaspoon of cinnamon
- ¼ teaspoon of baking soda
- ½ cup and 2 tablespoons of coconut flour
- ¼ cup of honey
- ¼ cup of coconut oil, softened
- 1 teaspoon of vanilla

Instructions

1. Heat your oven to 350 degrees F.
2. Add all the dry ingredients into a bowl and mix. Add all the wet ingredients into a different bowl and mix it together.
3. Add the wet ingredients into the bowl with the dry ingredients.

4. Use your fingers to spread the dough equally in a tart pan or a 9-inch pie pan.
5. If using a pie pan, allow it to bake for approximately 15 minutes, while the tart pan will bake for approximately 7 minutes.
6. If your filling does not require baking, take out of the oven, allow to cool down before you add the filling.
7. If you want to bake the filling, allow the crust to bake for about 5 to 7 minutes or until it turns lightly golden.
8. Put the crust in the freezer for approximately 30 minutes, then add the filling and put back into the oven.
9. You may cover the sides to avoid it getting burnt easily.

Chapter 4: Conclusion

It can be discouraging and frustrating when you make attempts to lose weight and do not see any improvement. You must understand your body type and the challenges that endomorphic people face. This understanding will help you to meet your weight loss and fitness goals.

Continue with low consumption of refined carbs, carry out physical activities regularly, and maintain portion control. These rules apply to just about everyone who wants to stay healthy and not just for the endomorphic bodies. Sticking with this routine righteously will help you to lose excess weight and keep the shedded weight out.

Other Books by Nancy Peterson

- CELIAC/ COELIAC DISEASE AND THE GLUTEN-FREE DIET: The Adult and Children's Guide to Live Pain-Free. https://amzn.to/2O2b8MP
- HERBAL MEDICINE. The Beginner's Guide: Natural Remedies for Healing Common Ailments with Medicinal Herbs https://amzn.to/2t0VB8w
- THE GALLBLADDER DIET: Foods to Eat, Causes, Diagnosis, Tips for Recovery & Prevention and Natural Remedies to Cure Gallstones without Surgery https://amzn.to/313cTi6
- CELERY JUICE: The Natural Medicine for Healing Your Body and Weight Loss (Contains Secret Celery Recipes) https://amzn.to/2tTiISQ
- ALKALINE PLANT-BASED DIET FOR BEGINNERS: Your Complete Guide for Weight Loss, Boost Your Energy, and

Cleanse Your Body with the Alkaline Diet. https://amzn.to/3aPZrSX
- LOW CALORIES DIET PLAN: Foods to Eat to Lose Weight and Stay Healthy. Includes 1,200 to 1,700-Calorie Meal Plans https://amzn.to/37vVyk1
- THE DIVERTICULITIS GUIDE TO LIVE PAIN-FREE: Diverticulitis Diet Plan, Foods to Eat & Avoid, Diagnosis and Tips for Causes, Recovery and Prevention https://amzn.to/38HTu8U
- Renal Diet Cookbook https://www.amazon.com/dp/B0849YJF5K
- Pescatarian Diet Plan and Cookbook https://www.amazon.com/dp/B085F3VR8D

Printed in Great Britain
by Amazon